T0019672

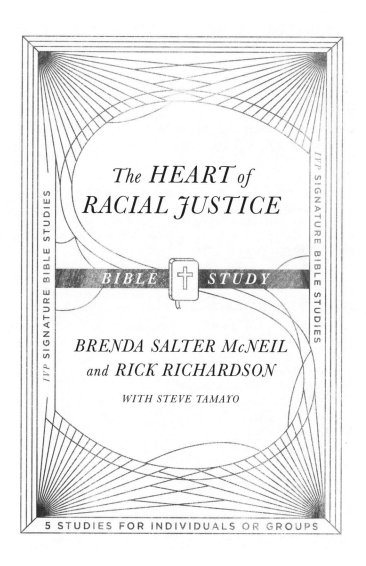

The HEART of RACIAL JUSTICE

IVP SIGNATURE BIBLE STUDIES

BIBLE ✝ *STUDY*

BRENDA SALTER McNEIL
and RICK RICHARDSON

WITH STEVE TAMAYO

5 STUDIES FOR INDIVIDUALS OR GROUPS

An imprint of InterVarsity Press
Downers Grove, Illinois

InterVarsity Press
P.O. Box 1400, Downers Grove, IL 60515-1426
ivpress.com
email@ivpress.com

This study guide adapts material from The Heart of Racial Justice, *expanded edition ©2009 by Brenda Salter McNeil and Rick Richardson, first edition ©2004 by Brenda Salter McNeil and Rick Richardson.*

InterVarsity Press® is the book-publishing division of InterVarsity Christian Fellowship/USA®, a movement of students and faculty active on campus at hundreds of universities, colleges, and schools of nursing in the United States of America, and a member movement of the International Fellowship of Evangelical Students. For information about local and regional activities, visit intervarsity.org.

While any stories in this book are true, some names and identifying information may have been changed to protect the privacy of individuals.

Cover design and image composite: David Fassett
Interior design: Daniel van Loon
Images: image of heart: © marek-studzinski / unsplash
    glittering gold background: © MirageC / Moment Collection / Getty Images

ISBN 978-0-8308-4849-2 (print)
ISBN 978-0-8308-4850-8 (digital)

Printed in the United States of America ∞

InterVarsity Press is committed to ecological stewardship and to the conservation of natural resources in all our operations. This book was printed using sustainably sourced paper.

Library of Congress Cataloging-in-Publication Data
Names: McNeil, Brenda Salter, 1955- author. | Richardson, Rick, 1955- author. | Tamayo, Steve, 1982- author.
Title: The heart of racial justice Bible study / Brenda Salter McNeil and Rick Richardson with Steve Tamayo.
Description: Downers Grove, IL : InterVarsity Press, 2021. | Series: IVP signature Bible studies |
    Includes bibliographical references.
Identifiers: LCCN 2021042643 (print) | LCCN 2021042644 (ebook) | ISBN 9780830848492 (print) |
    ISBN 9780830848508 (digital)
Subjects: LCSH: Race relations—Religious aspects—Christianity—Textbooks. | Reconciliation—Religious
    aspects—Christianity—Textbooks.
Classification: LCC BT734.2 .M363 2021 (print) | LCC BT734.2 (ebook) | DDC 241/.675—dc23
LC record available at https://lccn.loc.gov/2021042643
LC ebook record available at https://lccn.loc.gov/2021042644

P 21 20 19 18 17 16 15 14 13 12 11 10 9 8 7 6 5 4 3 2 1
Y 40 39 38 37 36 35 34 33 32 31 30 29 28 27 26 25 24 23 22

CONTENTS

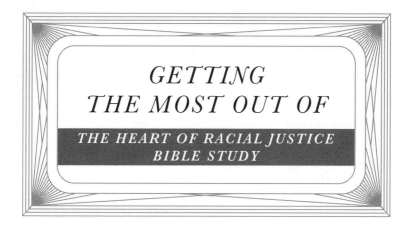

GETTING
THE MOST OUT OF
THE HEART OF RACIAL JUSTICE
BIBLE STUDY

KNOWING CHRIST is where faith begins. From there we are shaped through the essentials of discipleship: Bible study, prayer, Christian community, worship, and much more. We learn to grow in Christlike character, pursue justice, and share our faith with others. We persevere through doubts and gain wisdom for daily life. These are the topics woven into the IVP Signature Bible Studies. Working through this series will help you practice the essentials by exploring biblical truths found in classic books.

HOW IT'S PUT TOGETHER

Each session includes an opening quotation and suggested reading from the book *The Heart of Racial Justice*, a session goal to help guide your study, reflection questions to stir your thoughts on the topic, the text of the Bible passage, questions for exploring the passage, response questions to help you apply what you've learned, and a closing suggestion for prayer.

The workbook format is ideal for personal study and also allows group members to prepare in advance for discussions and record discussion notes. The responses you write here can form a permanent record of your thoughts and spiritual progress.

Throughout the guide are study-note sidebars that may be useful for group leaders or individuals. These notes do not give the answers, but they do provide additional background information on certain questions and can challenge participants to think deeper or differently about the content.

WHAT KIND OF GUIDE IS THIS?

The studies are not designed to merely tell you what one person thinks. Instead, through inductive study, they will help you discover for yourself what Scripture is saying. Each study deals with a particular passage—rather than jumping around the Bible—so that you can really delve into the biblical author's meaning in that context.

The studies ask three different kinds of questions about the Bible passage:

* *Observation* questions help you to understand the content of the passage by asking about the basic facts: who, what, when, where, and how.

* *Interpretation* questions delve into the meaning of the passage.

* *Application* questions help you discover implications for growing in Christ in your own life.

These three keys unlock the treasures of the biblical writings and help you live them out.

This is a thought-provoking guide. Each question assumes a variety of answers. Many questions do not have "right" answers, particularly questions that aim at meaning or application. Instead, the questions should inspire readers to explore the passage more thoroughly.

This study guide is flexible. You can use it for individual study, but it is also great for a variety of groups—student, professional, neighborhood, or church groups. Each study takes about forty-five minutes in a group setting or thirty minutes in personal study.

SUGGESTIONS FOR INDIVIDUAL STUDY

1. This guide is based on a classic book that will enrich your spiritual life. If you have not read *The Heart of Racial Justice*, you may want to read the portion recommended in the "Read" section before you begin your study. The ideas in the book will enhance your study, but the Bible text will be the focus of each session.

2. Begin each session with prayer, asking God to speak to you from his Word about this particular topic.

3. As you read the Scripture passage, reproduced for you from the New International Version, you may wish to mark phrases that seem important. Note in the margin any questions that come to your mind.

4. Close with the suggested prayer found at the end of each session. Speak to God about insights you have gained. Tell him of any desires you have for specific growth. Ask him to help you attempt to live out the principles described in that passage. You may wish to write your own prayer in this guide or a journal.

SUGGESTIONS FOR GROUP MEMBERS

Joining a Bible study group can be a great avenue to spiritual growth. Here are a few guidelines that will help you as you participate in the studies in this guide.

1. Reading the recommended portion of *The Heart of Racial Justice*, before or after each session, will enhance your study and understanding of the themes in this guide.

2. These studies use methods of inductive Bible study, which focuses on a particular passage of Scripture and works on it in depth. So try to dive into the given text instead of referring to other Scripture passages.

3. Questions are designed to help a group discuss together a passage of Scripture in order to understand its content, meaning, and implications. Most people are either natural talkers or natural listeners, yet this type of study works best if all members participate more or less evenly. Try to curb any natural tendency toward either excessive talking or excessive quiet. You and the rest of the group will benefit!

4. Most questions in this guide allow for a variety of answers. If you disagree with someone else's comment, gently say so. Then explain your own point of view from the passage before you.

5. Be willing to lead a discussion, if asked. Much of the preparation for leading has already been accomplished in the writing of this guide.

6. Respect the privacy of people in your group. Many people share things within the context of a Bible study group that they do not want to be public knowledge. Assume that personal information spoken within the group setting is private, unless you are specifically told otherwise.

7. We recommend that all groups agree on a few basic guidelines. You may wish to adapt this list to your situation:

   a. Anything said in this group is considered confidential and will not be discussed outside the group unless specific permission is given to do so.

   b. We will provide time for each person present to talk if he or she feels comfortable doing so.

    c. We will talk about ourselves and our own situations, avoiding conversation about other people.

    d. We will listen attentively to each other.

    e. We will pray for each other.

8. Enjoy your study. Prepare to grow!

SUGGESTIONS FOR GROUP LEADERS

There are specific suggestions to help you in the "Leading a Small Group" section. It describes how to lead a group discussion, gives helpful tips on group dynamics, and suggests ways to deal with problems that may arise during the discussion. With such helps, someone with little or no experience can lead an effective group study. Read this section carefully, even if you are leading only one group meeting.

INTRODUCTION

CHANGING HEARTS

TWO PRIMARY MODELS HAVE BEEN USED by great people of faith in America to overcome the racial divisions and inequities of our society. The first is what we refer to as the *relational* or *interpersonal model*. It can be summarized this way: Make a friend with someone from another race or ethnicity and you will bring about social change through friendship, one life at a time. This model seeks to address the isolation and ignorance that feed racism and injustice by encouraging interracial friendships that will dismantle inequality and discrimination over time.

This relational model has several strengths. First of all, it is feasible. You don't have to be an expert in racial and ethnic reconciliation to do it. Such simplicity can be extremely motivating for people who are newly interested in the ministry of reconciliation and need a realistic way to get started. The relational model also fits the basic worldview of many evangelical Christians, who understand the gospel in individual and interpersonal terms.

But it is not an adequate change strategy because it has nothing to say about the historical impact of sin and evil and the way this history has led to structural injustice that cannot be changed by the "one life at a time" approach. In addition, the friendship model does not bring adequate spiritual resources to bear on the immense problems of injustice, rage, guilt, shame, and deep woundedness. The depth of pain and hurt go far beyond what most relationships can absorb. Without profoundly spiritual, and even miraculous, intervention and healing many cross-ethnic interpersonal relationships are doomed to a constant cycle of frustration, misunderstanding, and further wounding. Developing a personal friendship with someone of another ethnicity is still probably the most important first step we can take, but it's not an adequate change model to address the immense challenges we face.

The second paradigm is what we call the *institutional change model.* This method seeks to create justice and equity by redistributing power among groups. Advocates of this approach would support hiring more people of color within an organization, mobilizing people to vote, using economic power through boycotts, job training, community organizing, public school reform, and the like. There are definite strengths to this proactive model. First of all, it encourages people to take responsibility for their own destiny. It empowers them with knowledge and skills to make new choices for their future. It is also realistic and takes into account the sociopolitical history that often works against reconciliation, justice, and equity.

The problem with this model, however, is that it reduces all relationships to relations of power. The kingdom of God is about more than group competition for power. The biblical ethic of love moves beyond human connections built solely on competition for power. The answer is not merely to reverse the roles and rules of the game. The goal is not merely to give the poor, oppressed, and wounded the upper hand. We need new rules and roles, and a new partnership that is not focused on who is the top dog and who is the underdog. Our goal is to be transformed toward God's multiethnic kingdom of worship and *shalom*, which is the Hebrew word for "God's peace with justice." The institutional change model is inadequate to accomplish this because it does not address the transformation of the human heart.

In the face of these limitations in our present models, we have been seeking a new approach and have turned to the ministry of healing. We have adapted and applied biblical, pastoral, spiritual, and psychological insights from the ministry of healing to problems of racial and ethnic division and hurt. For relationships to change, hearts must change. Here's how Oscar Romero, the late archbishop of El Salvador and an outstanding spiritual leader and advocate for peace and social justice, describes the need for change to begin with the human heart:

> How easy it is to denounce structural injustice, institutionalized violence, social sin! And it is true, this sin is everywhere, but where are the roots of this social sin? In the heart of every human being. Present day society is a sort of anonymous world in which no one is willing to admit guilt, and everyone is responsible. We are all sinners, and we have contributed to this massive crime and violence in our country. Salvation begins with the human person, with human dignity, with saving every person from sin. And in Lent this is God's call: Be converted!*

That is why the model we propose focuses on changing hearts and transforming lives—first of individual people, and then of whole communities.

---

*Oscar Romero, "A Pastor's Last Homily," *Sojourners*, May 1980, quoted in Marie Dennis, Renny Golden, and Scott Wright, *Oscar Romero: Reflections on His Life and Writings* (Maryknoll, NY: Orbis, 2000), 101.

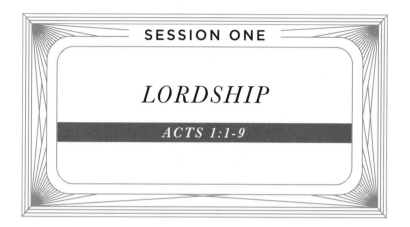

LORDSHIP

ACTS 1:1-9

JESUS CHRIST ASKS US TO SURRENDER absolutely everything, but in so doing he does not wipe out our ethnic identity. He forces us to affirm that our identity with him is the most salient. This is echoed by the apostle Paul in Galatians 3:28: "There is neither Jew nor Gentile, neither slave nor free, nor is there male and female, for you are all one in Christ Jesus."

Unfortunately, some people have wrongly interpreted this text to mean that culture and gender are irrelevant to our ultimate identity and relationships in the kingdom of God. We believe that in the kingdom there is no longer Jew or Greek, male or female, or any other dividing distinctions—but not because those aspects of our personhood are erased. Instead they are deepened and transcended. We become more than male and female, more than our ethnicity, culture, or nationality—never less. The future vision of the kingdom is the *fulfillment* of our race, culture, and gender, not their *erasure*.

SESSION GOAL	READ
Commit to the lordship of Jesus Christ by pursuing a lifestyle of personal, ethnic, and racial reconciliation.	Introduction and chapters one through three of *The Heart of Racial Justice*

REFLECT

✳ How would you identify your race, culture, or ethnic heritage?

✳ What experiences have you had with people from cultures different from your own?

STUDY

READ ACTS 1:1-9

¹In my former book, Theophilus, I wrote about all that Jesus began to do and to teach ²until the day he was taken up to heaven, after giving instructions through the Holy Spirit to the apostles he had chosen. ³After his suffering, he presented himself to them and gave many convincing proofs that he was alive. He appeared to them over a period of forty days and spoke about the kingdom of God. ⁴On one occasion, while he was eating with them, he gave them this command: "Do not leave Jerusalem, but wait for the gift my Father promised, which you have heard me speak about. ⁵For John baptized with water, but in a few days you will be baptized with the Holy Spirit."

⁶Then they gathered around him and asked him, "Lord, are you at this time going to restore the kingdom to Israel?"

⁷He said to them: "It is not for you to know the times or dates the Father has set by his own authority. ⁸But you will receive power when the Holy Spirit comes on you; and you will be my witnesses in Jerusalem, and in all Judea and Samaria, and to the ends of the earth."

⁹After he said this, he was taken up before their very eyes, and a cloud hid him from their sight.

1. What do the disciples ask Jesus?

2. Why might the disciples have asked Jesus about the kingdom?

"God's kingdom was the dominant theme in Jesus' teaching. . . . Graeme Goldsworthy, in his book *Gospel and Kingdom*, helpfully presents the kingdom as the binding theme of the whole Bible . . . [defining] the kingdom as 'God's people in God's place under God's rule.'"*

3. How do the disciples betray their ethnocentric focus?

4. How does Jesus respond to the disciples?

5. What might the disciples have felt about the people who lived in each of the places Jesus mentions?

Jerusalem was the center of the world for Jesus' Jewish disciples, given the location of the temple and the history of Israel. At the same time, the religious and political leadership in Jerusalem had executed Jesus. Jesus' followers grew up in Galilee, a region in Judea outside of Jerusalem.

6. How do you think the disciples might have felt about this commission?

7. Why might Jesus have mentioned "power" in this passage?

Racial and ethnic reconciliation will be a
distinguishing mark, maybe even *the* distinguishing
mark, of this next outpouring of God's Spirit.

 **RESPOND**

✳ What does this passage say to you about who God has called
you to reach?

✳ Consider the spiritual communities to which you belong. In
what ways has your group chosen to only care about people
from your background?

✳ How might God be calling you to change in response to the
lordship of Christ?

⫸ PRAY ⫷

Thank the Lord for giving you a racial, cultural, and ethnic heritage. Tell him you're ready to submit every facet of your heritage to his will. Ask him to show you how he wants you to change.

---

*Vaughan Roberts, *God's Big Picture* (Downers Grove, IL: InterVarsity Press, 2002), 21.

SCRIPTURE

ACTS 6:1-7

IN PREPARING TO TEACH A SEMINAR on the book of Acts together, we discovered some interesting things about ourselves. As we wrestled with Acts 2, Brenda kept pointing out the multiethnic and multicultural dimensions of this text. She said that it was not by accident that God revealed his Spirit and proclaimed the gospel to Jewish converts who were from many nations and spoke many different languages.

Rick, on the other hand, felt that she was making too big an issue of the cultural and ethnic dimensions. He believed that the disciples spoke in many tongues because it was necessary for them to communicate the gospel to the different people who had gathered in Jerusalem. In his view, God was just making a strategic evangelistic and communication move. The diversity of language and the diversity of the first community were a means to an end: reaching all the individuals present with the good news about Jesus.

Brenda kept seeing more significance to the makeup of this first church. She emphasized that the gospel is not only a message about saving individuals but also a message about reconciling the nations. Thus, the *gospel proclamation* was accompanied by a *reconciled community*—a sign that God was at work.

We have begun to think that even in our day as well, a reconciled community may be the sign of the in-breaking kingdom of God.

SESSION GOAL	READ
Commit to read Scripture with new eyes and to respond with a new heart to God's call for reconciliation.	Chapters four and five of *The Heart of Racial Justice*

REFLECT

✳ What stories of ethnic or racial reconciliation do you find inspiring?

✳ How important do you think racial and ethnic reconciliation are in the Scriptures? What passages come to mind?

STUDY

READ ACTS 6:1-7

[1]In those days when the number of disciples was increasing, the Hellenistic Jews among them complained against the Hebraic Jews because their widows were being overlooked in the daily distribution of food. [2]So the Twelve gathered

all the disciples together and said, "It would not be right for us to neglect the ministry of the word of God in order to wait on tables. ³Brothers and sisters, choose seven men from among you who are known to be full of the Spirit and wisdom. We will turn this responsibility over to them ⁴and will give our attention to prayer and the ministry of the word."

⁵This proposal pleased the whole group. They chose Stephen, a man full of faith and of the Holy Spirit; also Philip, Procorus, Nicanor, Timon, Parmenas, and Nicolas from Antioch, a convert to Judaism. ⁶They presented these men to the apostles, who prayed and laid their hands on them.

⁷So the word of God spread. The number of disciples in Jerusalem increased rapidly, and a large number of priests became obedient to the faith.

1. What problem is the early church experiencing?

2. How is this an ethnic or cultural issue?

3. How do the disciples solve the problem?

4. What are the characteristics of the men they choose to solve
   the problem?

> The names of these men are Greek names, not
> Hebrew names. So Hellenistic Jews, who were
> considered less pure than Hebraic Jews, were
> given the task of serving all the widows.

5. Why might the ethnic or cultural heritage of these men
   matter for the narrative?

> "A church cannot be truly missionary if it
> does not do justice to those who come
> to it as a result of that mission."*

6. Why might Luke (the author of Acts) have gone out of his way to highlight the ethnic contours of the conflict?

7. How does the resolution of this crisis affect the spread of the gospel?

It is imperative that the Christian church regain its integrity to address injustice. This will require that we relinquish the individualism and isolation that have been prevalent among evangelical Christians in the past, so that we can develop new models of racial reconciliation, social justice, and spiritual healing. Our unity and reconciliation efforts could be the greatest witness of the church to the power of the gospel in the twenty-first century.

 **RESPOND**

✳ How might this model of sharing power and involving people in meeting their own needs help you reach the people God is calling you to reach?

✳ Have you ever read the Bible with these kinds of reconciliation questions in mind? Take time this week to look at how God uses Stephen and Philip in crosscultural ministry over the next several chapters of Acts.

PRAY

Confess the ways your heart and eyes have been closed to the suffering of others in this racially divided world. Ask God to give you eyes to see and hearts like his, full of a desire to see unity, reconciliation, and justice.

---

*Justo L. Gonzalez, *Acts: The Gospel of the Spirit* (Maryknoll, NY: Orbis Books, 2001), 94.

PRAYER

ACTS 10:1-48

RICK LED A CONCERT OF PRAYER at Moody Memorial Church, a large evangelical church that was founded in downtown Chicago by the famous nineteenth-century evangelist D. L. Moody. The group that met for prayer represented eleven different denominations, including Lutheran, Methodist, Episcopalian, Baptist, and Pentecostal. The more than twelve hundred people who gathered for prayer were Black, White, Latino, Native American, and Asian, with some visiting from other nations. This diverse group of people held two things in common: a commitment to the lordship of Christ and a dedication to reach the city with the gospel.

The worship began with prayers given in Spanish, Yoruba, Korean, and English. The group celebrated to the beat of salsa music and sang contemporary choruses. When a gospel choir led the worship, it felt as if the whole congregation would rise through the roof with praise because God was so powerfully present. These people experienced a unity with one another that honored their different ethnicities and races in a way that is rare in our world. They were being knit together by the Holy Spirit in worship.

SESSION GOAL	READ
Commit to prayer by listening to God and asking to be filled with the Spirit to empower you for reconciliation.	Chapters six through eight of *The Heart of Racial Justice*

REFLECT

✳ What's been your experience with God speaking to you?

✳ When have you felt weary, overwhelmed, or confused in your pursuit of racial reconciliation?

STUDY

READ ACTS 10:1-48

¹At Caesarea there was a man named Cornelius, a centurion in what was known as the Italian Regiment. ²He and all his family were devout and God-fearing; he gave generously to those in need and prayed to God regularly. ³One day at about three in the afternoon he had a vision. He distinctly saw an angel of God, who came to him and said, "Cornelius!"

⁴Cornelius stared at him in fear. "What is it, Lord?" he asked. The angel answered, "Your prayers and gifts to the poor have come up as a memorial offering before God. ⁵Now send men to Joppa to bring back a man named Simon who is called Peter. ⁶He is staying with Simon the tanner, whose house is by the sea."

⁷When the angel who spoke to him had gone, Cornelius called two of his servants and a devout soldier who was one of his attendants. ⁸He told them everything that had happened and sent them to Joppa.

⁹About noon the following day as they were on their journey and approaching the city, Peter went up on the roof to pray. ¹⁰He became hungry and wanted something to eat, and while the meal was being prepared, he fell into a trance. ¹¹He saw heaven opened and something like a large sheet being let down to earth by its four corners. ¹²It contained all kinds of four-footed animals, as well as reptiles and birds. ¹³Then a voice told him, "Get up, Peter. Kill and eat."

¹⁴"Surely not, Lord!" Peter replied. "I have never eaten anything impure or unclean."

¹⁵The voice spoke to him a second time, "Do not call anything impure that God has made clean."

¹⁶This happened three times, and immediately the sheet was taken back to heaven.

¹⁷While Peter was wondering about the meaning of the vision, the men sent by Cornelius found out where Simon's house was and stopped at the gate. ¹⁸They called out, asking if Simon who was known as Peter was staying there.

¹⁹While Peter was still thinking about the vision, the Spirit said to him, "Simon, three men are looking for you.

²⁰So get up and go downstairs. Do not hesitate to go with them, for I have sent them."

²¹Peter went down and said to the men, "I'm the one you're looking for. Why have you come?"

²²The men replied, "We have come from Cornelius the centurion. He is a righteous and God-fearing man, who is respected by all the Jewish people. A holy angel told him to ask you to come to his house so that he could hear what you have to say." ²³Then Peter invited the men into the house to be his guests.

The next day Peter started out with them, and some of the believers from Joppa went along. ²⁴The following day he arrived in Caesarea. Cornelius was expecting them and had called together his relatives and close friends. ²⁵As Peter entered the house, Cornelius met him and fell at his feet in reverence. ²⁶But Peter made him get up. "Stand up," he said, "I am only a man myself."

²⁷While talking with him, Peter went inside and found a large gathering of people. ²⁸He said to them: "You are well aware that it is against our law for a Jew to associate with or visit a Gentile. But God has shown me that I should not call anyone impure or unclean. ²⁹So when I was sent for, I came without raising any objection. May I ask why you sent for me?"

³⁰Cornelius answered: "Three days ago I was in my house praying at this hour, at three in the afternoon. Suddenly a man in shining clothes stood before me ³¹and said, 'Cornelius, God has heard your prayer and remembered your gifts to the poor. ³²Send to Joppa for Simon who is called Peter. He is a guest in the home of Simon the tanner, who lives by the sea.' ³³So I sent for you immediately, and

it was good of you to come. Now we are all here in the presence of God to listen to everything the Lord has commanded you to tell us."

³⁴Then Peter began to speak: "I now realize how true it is that God does not show favoritism ³⁵but accepts from every nation the one who fears him and does what is right. ³⁶You know the message God sent to the people of Israel, announcing the good news of peace through Jesus Christ, who is Lord of all. ³⁷You know what has happened throughout the province of Judea, beginning in Galilee after the baptism that John preached—³⁸how God anointed Jesus of Nazareth with the Holy Spirit and power, and how he went around doing good and healing all who were under the power of the devil, because God was with him.

³⁹"We are witnesses of everything he did in the country of the Jews and in Jerusalem. They killed him by hanging him on a cross, ⁴⁰but God raised him from the dead on the third day and caused him to be seen. ⁴¹He was not seen by all the people, but by witnesses whom God had already chosen—by us who ate and drank with him after he rose from the dead. ⁴²He commanded us to preach to the people and to testify that he is the one whom God appointed as judge of the living and the dead. ⁴³All the prophets testify about him that everyone who believes in him receives forgiveness of sins through his name."

⁴⁴While Peter was still speaking these words, the Holy Spirit came on all who heard the message. ⁴⁵The circumcised believers who had come with Peter were astonished that the gift of the Holy Spirit had been poured out even on Gentiles. ⁴⁶For they heard them speaking in tongues and praising God.

Then Peter said, [47]"Surely no one can stand in the way of their being baptized with water. They have received the Holy Spirit just as we have." [48]So he ordered that they be baptized in the name of Jesus Christ. Then they asked Peter to stay with them for a few days.

1. What do we know about Cornelius, why God chose him, and what he was doing when he heard from God?

2. What do Cornelius and Peter have in common?

3. In what ways does Peter's vision differ from Cornelius's?

4. Why might God have given the men such different visions?

5. What do you notice about Peter's interactions with the men who came to give him Cornelius's message?

"It is difficult for us to grasp the impassible gulf which yawned in those days between the Jews on the one hand and the Gentiles (including even the 'God-fearers') on the other. . . . Israel twisted the doctrine of election into one of favouritism, became filled with racial pride and hatred, despised Gentiles as 'dogs,' and developed traditions which kept them apart. No orthodox Jew would ever enter the home of a Gentile, even a God-fearer, or invite such into his home (see verse 28)."*

6. How do Cornelius and Peter respond to what God is doing supernaturally?

7. What role do Peter and Cornelius's cultural backgrounds play in the story? In what ways is their behavior shaped by or in contrast to their ethnic heritage?

8. How does this interaction change Cornelius and Peter?

> When a person converts to Jesus Christ, it is
> always a personal *and* social act—a radical
> switch of allegiances between kingdoms.

 RESPOND

✳ Identify one person from an ethnic community different from your own and one systemic issue their community cares about. Intercede for them this week.

✳ Take some time this week to sit quietly and listen to the Lord. Put your phone in airplane mode. Find a place where you can have some silence and privacy. Speak these words aloud—"Speak, Lord. I'm listening"—then wait. Write down what comes to your mind and share it with a trusted friend or someone from your group.

⟫⟫⟫ PRAY ⟪⟪⟪

Ask God to speak to you this week. Ask the Lord to give you ears to hear him and a heart filled with his light and love. Ask to be filled with God's Spirit that you might meet God-given needs in God-glorifying ways.

---

*John Stott, *The Message of Acts* (Downers Grove, IL: InterVarsity Press, 1990), 185.

IN ORDER FOR POTENTIAL RECONCILERS to move from ignorance and isolation into a lifestyle of racial and ethnic reconciliation, they must develop ongoing partnerships that support their desire and commitment to be people God can use in the healing of people and nations. It is critical that people begin to live out what they believe about racial and ethnic reconciliation in their daily lives, choice of friends, place of worship, and economic and political decisions.

These behaviors, exercised consistently over an extended period of time, are what establish racial and ethnic reconciliation as an authentic core value in the life of a person or group. Ongoing partnerships create a context in which trust is developed—a level of trust that allows people to challenge and support each other on tough issues regarding the use of their influence to promote justice and equality for all people. Together, as a community of faith, they make a commitment to extend themselves into the world to create structures and systems that promote peace, justice, and reconciliation for people of every nationality.

SESSION GOAL	READ
Commit to community by building relationships that nurture your commitment to racial and ethnic reconciliation.	Chapter nine of *The Heart of Racial Justice*

 **REFLECT**

✳ Look around your church, fellowship, or small group. What racial, ethnic, or cultural communities do you see represented?

✳ Who do you feel is missing from your community?

 **STUDY**

READ ACTS 11:19-30

[19]Now those who had been scattered by the persecution that broke out when Stephen was killed traveled as far as Phoenicia, Cyprus and Antioch, spreading the word only among Jews. [20]Some of them, however, men from Cyprus and Cyrene, went to Antioch and began to speak to Greeks also, telling them the good news about the Lord Jesus. [21]The Lord's hand was with them, and a great number of people believed and turned to the Lord.

²²News of this reached the church in Jerusalem, and they sent Barnabas to Antioch. ²³When he arrived and saw what the grace of God had done, he was glad and encouraged them all to remain true to the Lord with all their hearts. ²⁴He was a good man, full of the Holy Spirit and faith, and a great number of people were brought to the Lord.

²⁵Then Barnabas went to Tarsus to look for Saul, ²⁶and when he found him, he brought him to Antioch. So for a whole year Barnabas and Saul met with the church and taught great numbers of people. The disciples were called Christians first at Antioch.

²⁷During this time some prophets came down from Jerusalem to Antioch. ²⁸One of them, named Agabus, stood up and through the Spirit predicted that a severe famine would spread over the entire Roman world. (This happened during the reign of Claudius.) ²⁹The disciples, as each one was able, decided to provide help for the brothers and sisters living in Judea. ³⁰This they did, sending their gift to the elders by Barnabas and Saul.

1. How did the church in Antioch begin, and who started it?

2. Why might the Jerusalem church feel a need to examine the church in Antioch?

3. What about Barnabas might have equipped him to engage and help lead the first truly multiethnic church?

Barnabas also shows up in Acts 4 (in contrast to Ananias and Sapphira) and Acts 9 (welcoming the newly converted Paul into the Jerusalem church).

4. Why do you think it was significant that the followers of Jesus were first called "Christians" in Antioch?

Although the term Christians (Greek *Christianoi*) "does not seem to have caught on initially, since elsewhere it appears only twice in the New Testament (Acts 26:28 and 1 Pet 4:16), it at least emphasized the Christ-centred nature of discipleship. For the word's formation was parallel to *Hērōdianoi* (Herodians) and *Kaisarianoi* (Caesar's people); it marked out the disciples as being above all the people, the followers, the servants of Christ."*

5. Why might the church in Antioch—rather than the church in Jerusalem—have earned this moniker?

READ ACTS 13:1-3 AND 14:26-28

13 ¹Now in the church at Antioch there were prophets and teachers: Barnabas, Simeon called Niger, Lucius of Cyrene, Manaen (who had been brought up with Herod the tetrarch) and Saul. ²While they were worshiping the Lord and fasting, the Holy Spirit said, "Set apart for me Barnabas and Saul for the work to which I have called them." ³So after they had fasted and prayed, they placed their hands on them and sent them off. . . .

14 ²⁶From Attalia [Barnabas and Saul] sailed back to Antioch, where they had been committed to the grace of God for the work they had now completed. ²⁷On arriving there, they gathered the church together and reported all that God had done through them and how he had opened a door of faith to the Gentiles. ²⁸And they stayed there a long time with the disciples.

6. How does the leadership structure in Antioch reflect the makeup of the church?

7. Why do you think God uses this church to launch Barnabas and Paul in mission to the Gentiles?

God calls each of us to play a different role in the battle for ethnic healing and racial justice. However, if racial and ethnic reconciliation is to become an ongoing reality in our world, we must all intentionally take some action steps in that direction. Therefore, we urge you to activate your commitment to racial and ethnic reconciliation by developing ongoing partnerships that will help you continue your growth as a reconciler, guard against burnout, and support your lifestyle of racial righteousness.

 **RESPOND**

✳ How would you like to see your group grow in becoming more like the Antioch church? How might this affect relationship decisions in your life?

✳ Identify one step you want to take to develop or deepen a cross-ethnic or crosscultural friendship. Pray for each other as a group (or, if using this study alone, ask a trusted friend to pray for you).

PRAY

Ask God to cleanse you of sentimental views of people, history, and Scripture. Receive the Spirit's power to change. Thank God that he's leading you to love in costly ways.

---

*John Stott, *The Message of Acts*, rev. ed. (Downers Grove, IL: InterVarsity Press, 2020), 187.

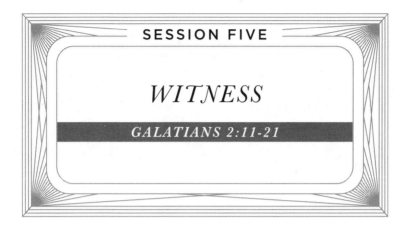

WITNESS

GALATIANS 2:11-21

WE DESPERATELY NEED A MARRIAGE between ministries of evangelism and ministries of racial reconciliation and justice. The proclamation and demonstration of the gospel *must* go together. People are tired of words that are not backed up by personal and social actions of compassion, service, and justice. People today want to experience the gospel and see its impact for personal and social transformation before they want to hear our spiritual viewpoint. They want to see a message that *works* before they will consider responding in their own lives. *Experience* for people today must precede *explanation* if we are to gain a hearing for the gospel.

As a result, many ministries today are pursuing compassion, service, and justice as their primary way to awaken spiritual interest in the hearts of seekers and skeptics. Combining reconciliation, justice, and evangelism efforts puts the gospel back together and connects to the hearts of people in a culture tired of words without praxis.

<table>
<tr><td>

SESSION GOAL

Commit to public witness by
sharing your heart for reconcili-
ation and standing up for racial
and ethnic justice.

</td><td>

READ

Chapter ten of
The Heart of Racial Justice

</td></tr>
</table>

 **REFLECT**

✴ Who do you know who has taken a costly stand for something he or she believed in?

✴ What comes to your mind when you hear "witness"?

 **STUDY**

SKIM GALATIANS 1:1–2:10, THEN READ 2:11-21

¹¹When Cephas came to Antioch, I opposed him to his
face, because he stood condemned. ¹²For before certain
men came from James, he used to eat with the Gentiles.
But when they arrived, he began to draw back and separate
himself from the Gentiles because he was afraid of those
who belonged to the circumcision group. ¹³The other Jews
joined him in his hypocrisy, so that by their hypocrisy even
Barnabas was led astray.

[14]When I saw that they were not acting in line with the truth of the gospel, I said to Cephas in front of them all, "You are a Jew, yet you live like a Gentile and not like a Jew. How is it, then, that you force Gentiles to follow Jewish customs?

[15]"We who are Jews by birth and not sinful Gentiles [16]know that a person is not justified by the works of the law, but by faith in Jesus Christ. So we, too, have put our faith in Christ Jesus that we may be justified by faith in Christ and not by the works of the law, because by the works of the law no one will be justified.

[17]"But if, in seeking to be justified in Christ, we Jews find ourselves also among the sinners, doesn't that mean that Christ promotes sin? Absolutely not! [18]If I rebuild what I destroyed, then I really would be a lawbreaker.

[19]"For through the law I died to the law so that I might live for God. [20]I have been crucified with Christ and I no longer live, but Christ lives in me. The life I now live in the body, I live by faith in the Son of God, who loved me and gave himself for me. [21]I do not set aside the grace of God, for if righteousness could be gained through the law, Christ died for nothing!"

1. What is the context of Galatians 2:11-21?

"The gospel is at stake in Galatians, for many
of the Galatians were beginning to turn, or
at least they were contemplating a turn,
away from Paul's gospel (Gal 1:6)."*

2. What conflict was Paul facing?

3. How do you think this conflict would make Paul feel?

4. Look at Peter's behavior. What might have motivated him?

James was the leader of the church in Jerusalem,
but it seems that the "certain men" who came to
Antioch did not actually represent the consensus
of the Jerusalem church (see Acts 15).

5. What impact would Peter's behavior have had on others?

6. Why does Paul see Peter's actions as a threat to the gospel and to Paul's life work?

7. How does Paul respond? What stands out to you?

8. What will happen to the gospel and to the centrality of Jesus' death on the cross if Paul lets Peter get away with separating himself culturally from the Greeks?

> Our God is a God of reconciliation. Ethnocentrism
> and racism always carry with them an
> understanding of salvation that violates the
> truth of the gospel and the necessity of the cross.
> Whenever our community reinforces splitting
> the new humanity back into its separate and
> alienated parts, the gospel has been undone!

 **RESPOND**

＊ What steps do you want to commit to in the long term to
make racial and ethnic reconciliation an ongoing part of
your life and your Christian community?

＊ How do you personally want to express your commitment
to ethnic and racial reconciliation?

⟶ PRAY ⟵

As you prepare to apply the spiritual model of ethnic healing and racial justice, pray with us the prayer that Jesus gave:

Our Father in heaven,
hallowed be your name.
Your kingdom come, your will be done,
on earth as it is in heaven.
Give us this day our daily bread,
And forgive us our debts, as we also have forgiven our
debtors.
And lead us not into temptation,
but deliver us from evil.
For yours is the kingdom, and the power, and the glory
forever.
Amen.

---

*Jarvis J. Williams, *One New Man* (Nashville: B&H Academic, 2010), 54.

LEADING A SMALL GROUP

LEADING A BIBLE DISCUSSION can be an enjoyable and rewarding experience. But it can also be intimidating—especially if you've never done it before. If this is how you feel, you're in good company.

Remember when God asked Moses to lead the Israelites out of Egypt? Moses replied, "Please send someone else" (Exodus 4:13)! But God gave Moses the help (human and divine) he needed to be a strong leader.

Leading a Bible discussion is not difficult if you follow certain guidelines. You don't need to be an expert on the Bible or a trained teacher. The suggestions listed below can help you to effectively fulfill your role as leader—and enjoy doing it.

PREPARING FOR THE STUDY

1. As you study the passage before the group meeting, ask God to help you understand it and apply it in your own life. Unless this happens, you will not be prepared to lead others. Pray too for the various members of the group. Ask God to open your hearts to the message of his Word and motivate you to action.

2. Read the introduction to the entire guide to get an overview of the subject at hand and the issues that will be explored.

3. Be ready to respond to the "Reflect" questions with a personal story or example. The group will be only as vulnerable and open as its leader.

4. Read the chapters of the companion book that are recommended at the beginning of the session.

5. Read and reread the assigned Bible passage to familiarize yourself with it. You may want to look up the passage in a Bible so that you can see its context.

6. This study guide is based on the New International Version of the Bible. It will help you and the group if you use this translation as the basis for your study and discussion.

7. Carefully work through each question in the study. Spend time in meditation and reflection as you consider how to respond.

8. Write your thoughts and responses in the space provided in the study guide. This will help you to express your understanding of the passage clearly.

9. It might help you to have a Bible dictionary handy. Use it to look up any unfamiliar words, names, or places.

10. Take the final (application) study questions and the "Respond" portion of each study seriously. Consider what this means for your life, what changes you may need to make in your lifestyle, or what actions you can take in your church or with people you know. Remember that the group will follow your lead in responding to the studies.

LEADING THE STUDY

1. Be sure everyone in your group has a study guide and a Bible. Encourage the group to prepare beforehand for each discussion by reading the introduction to the guide and by working through the questions for that session.

2. At the beginning of your first time together, explain that these studies are meant to be discussions, not lectures. Encourage the members of the group to participate. However, do not put pressure on those who may be hesitant to speak during the first few sessions.

3. Begin the study on time. Open with prayer, asking God to help the group understand and apply the passage.

4. Have a group member read aloud the introductory paragraphs at the beginning of the discussion. This will remind the group of the topic of the study.

5. Discuss the "Reflect" questions before reading the Bible passage. These kinds of opening questions are important for several reasons. First, there is usually a stiffness that needs to be overcome before people will begin to talk openly. A good question will break the ice.

Second, most people will have lots of different things going on in their minds (dinner, an exam, an important meeting coming up, how to get the car fixed), which have nothing to do with the study. A creative question will get their attention and draw them into the discussion.

Third, opening questions can reveal where our thoughts or feelings need to be transformed by Scripture. That is why it is important not to read the passage before the "Reflect" questions are asked. The passage will tend to color the honest reactions people would otherwise give, because they feel they are supposed to think the way the Bible does.

6. Have a group member read aloud the Scripture passage.

7. As you ask the questions, keep in mind that they are designed to be used just as they are written. You may simply read them aloud. Or you may prefer to express them in your own words.

There may be times when it is appropriate to deviate from the study guide. For example, a question may already have been answered. If so, move on to the next question. Or someone may raise an important question not covered in the guide. Take time to discuss it, but try to keep the group from going off on tangents.

8. Avoid offering the first answer to a study question. Repeat or rephrase questions if necessary until they are clearly understood. An eager group quickly becomes passive and silent if members think the leader will give all the _right_ answers.

9. Don't be afraid of silence. People may need time to think about the question before formulating their answers.

10. Don't be content with just one answer. Ask, "What do the rest of you think?" or, "Anything else?" until several people have given answers to a question. You might point out one of the study sidebars to help spur discussion; for example, "Does the quotation on page seventeen provide any insight as you think about this question?"

11. Acknowledge all contributions. Be affirming whenever possible. Never reject an answer. If it is clearly off-base, ask, "Which verse led you to that conclusion?" or, "What do the rest of you think?"

12. Don't expect every answer to be addressed to you, even though this will probably happen at first. As group members become more at ease, they will begin to truly interact with each other. This is one sign of healthy discussion.

13. Don't be afraid of controversy. It can be stimulating! If you don't resolve an issue completely, don't be frustrated. Move on and keep it in mind for later. A subsequent study may solve the problem.

14. Try to periodically summarize what the group has said about the passage. This helps to draw together the various ideas mentioned and gives continuity to the study. But don't preach.

15. When you come to the application questions at the end of each "Study" section, be willing to keep the discussion going by describing how you have been affected by the study. It's important that we each apply the message of the passage to ourselves in a specific way.

Depending on the makeup of your group and the length of time you've been together, you may or may not want to discuss the "Respond" section. If not, allow the group to read it and reflect on it silently. Encourage members to make specific commitments and to write them in their study guide. Ask them the following week how they did with their commitments.

16. Conclude your time together with conversational prayer. Ask for God's help in following through on the commitments you've made.

17. End the group discussion on time.

Many more suggestions and helps are found in The Big Book on Small Groups *by Jeffrey Arnold.*

THE IVP SIGNATURE COLLECTION

Since 1947 InterVarsity Press has been publishing thoughtful Christian books that serve the university, the church, and the world. In celebration of our seventy-fifth anniversary, IVP is releasing special editions of select iconic and bestselling books from throughout our history.

RELEASED IN 2019

Basic Christianity (1958)
JOHN STOTT

How to Give Away Your Faith (1966)
PAUL E. LITTLE

RELEASED IN 2020

The God Who Is There (1968)
FRANCIS A. SCHAEFFER

This Morning with God (1968)
EDITED BY CAROL ADENEY AND BILL WEIMER

The Fight (1976)
JOHN WHITE

Free at Last? (1983)
CARL F. ELLIS JR.

The Dust of Death (1973)
OS GUINNESS

The Singer (1975)
CALVIN MILLER

RELEASED IN 2021

Knowing God (1973)
J. I. PACKER

Out of the Saltshaker and Into the World
(1979) REBECCA MANLEY PIPPERT

A Long Obedience in the Same Direction
(1980) EUGENE H. PETERSON

More Than Equals (1993)
SPENCER PERKINS AND CHRIS RICE

Between Heaven and Hell (1982)
PETER KREEFT

Good News About Injustice (1999)
GARY A. HAUGEN

The Challenge of Jesus (1999)
N. T. WRIGHT

Hearing God (1999)
DALLAS WILLARD

RELEASING IN 2022

The Heart of Racial Justice (2004)
BRENDA SALTER McNEIL AND
RICK RICHARDSON

Sacred Rhythms (2006)
RUTH HALEY BARTON

Habits of the Mind (2000)
JAMES W. SIRE

True Story (2008)
JAMES CHOUNG

Scribbling in the Sand (2002)
MICHAEL CARD

The Next Worship (2015)
SANDRA MARIA VAN OPSTAL

Delighting in the Trinity (2012)
MICHAEL REEVES

Strong and Weak (2016)
ANDY CROUCH

Liturgy of the Ordinary (2016)
TISH HARRISON WARREN

IVP SIGNATURE BIBLE STUDIES

As companions to the IVP Signature Collection, IVP Signature Bible Studies feature the inductive study method, equipping individuals and groups to explore the biblical truths embedded in these books.

Basic Christianity Bible Study
JOHN STOTT

How to Give Away Your Faith Bible Study
PAUL E. LITTLE

The Singer Bible Study, CALVIN MILLER

Knowing God Bible Study, J. I. PACKER

A Long Obedience in the Same Direction Bible Study, EUGENE H. PETERSON

Good News About Injustice Bible Study
GARY A. HAUGEN

Hearing God Bible Study
DALLAS WILLARD

The Heart of Racial Justice Bible Study
BRENDA SALTER McNEIL AND
RICK RICHARDSON

True Story Bible Study, JAMES CHOUNG

The Next Worship Bible Study
SANDRA MARIA VAN OPSTAL

Strong and Weak Bible Study
ANDY CROUCH

ALSO AVAILABLE

FOREWORD BY EUGENE CHO

BRENDA SALTER McNEIL

With contributions by J. DEREK McNEIL

ROADMAP TO RECONCILIATION 2.0

MOVING COMMUNITIES INTO UNITY, WHOLENESS AND JUSTICE